MIND CHANGE HANDBOOK

The Companion Guide To
Mind Change: Changing The World One Mind At A Time

MIND CHANGE, LLC

Copyright © 2019 Mind Change, LLC

Written and Created by Kent & Heather McKean

All rights reserved. No part of this book may be reproduced by any mechanical, photographic, or electronic process; nor may it be stored in a retrieval system transmitted, or otherwise be copied for public or private use without written consent from Mind Change LLC. "Fair Use" practices such as brief quotations in articles and reviews may be used with proper citation. Please ensure that you are compliant with current copyright laws by purchasing an authorized copy of this book.

The information, applications, and suggestions in this book are the results of years of research, personal experience, and client work. This book is intended to offer logical, scientific, and practical suggestions to help address negative thought patterns and outcomes. Nothing in this book is to be used as a replacement for professional medical or psychological help. Please discuss specific emotional or physical symptoms with your health care provider. Mind Change, LLC and the author make no guarantees or warranties that any individual will experience a particular result. Mind Change, LLC and the author disclaim any and all liability from the outcomes, direct or indirect, arising from the use or application of anything contained in this book. Mind Change is intended for educational purposes only.

Mind Change, LLC
PO Box 791377
Paia, HI 96779

ISBN: 978-1-7334220-1-7
www.MindChange.com

This handbook is dedicated to all of the wonderful people who have read and loved Mind Change. So many of you reached out to me and shared your experiences. Because of your invaluable feedback, this handbook was born! Thank you to all of you brave souls who are on the journey to your BEST LIFE. Special thanks to my Mind Change MasterMind Group and all their support and feedback. Big love to Tiffany Jeffers, Cara Ugolini, and Victoria Yamaguchi for building the bones of this book. Last but not least, my amazing family. Cadence, and Savannah…you all have cheered me along every step of the way. Kent, you are my partner in everything. My tech support, customer relations, videographer, editor, my partner, and "hardest worker ever" kind of guy. It does not go unseen. Thanks for making it all worth it.

TABLE OF CONTENTS

Introduction	1
Mind Change Manifesto	7
G. P. S.	25
Safe Haven	65
PaNE CuRe	75
Pattern Interrupt	97
Mind Change In Action	109
Bonus	129
Congratulations	138
Extra Notes	140

INTRODUCTION

Welcome to the *Mind Change* Companion Guide, and congratulations on investing in the most powerful resource of all, YOUR MIND! The journey within is not for the faint-hearted, so I have provided this book to support you as you embark on this great adventure.

*"If you can imagine it, you can achieve it.
If you can dream it, you can become it."
-William Arthur Ward*

This guide is based on the tools outlined in *Mind Change: Changing The World One Mind At A Time*. Specifically, this handbook follows Part 2 of *Mind Change*, and helps you walk through the Mind Change Method. Please review it entirely before attempting to use this guide.

Whether you are working with a practitioner or doing the work on your own, this guide contains tools to complete the process and begin to transform your mind!

This guide is broken down into separate sections with plenty of room to write, draw, post photos, cards, or anything your creative mind can come up with. Each section has a brief summary of the exercise and some prompts to get you started.

For a more detailed and rich understanding of each section, please refer back to Part 2 of *Mind Change*.

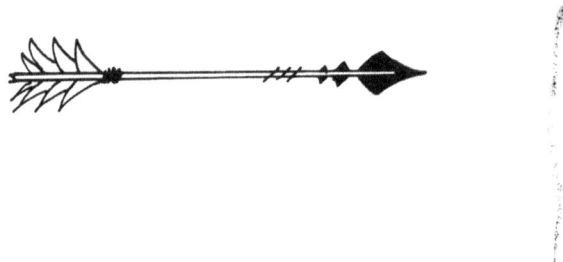

One of the most prominent overarching themes to "self-work" is almost always: Love. Love yourself enough to take the time and energy to invest in this process. AND, be loving to yourself in the process.

Remember, the things you want to change are a result of subconsciously "practicing" them for years, decades or generations! Some of these things may have been passed down over centuries. Having a Mind Change about your problem, life, or disease takes considerably less time to change than it did to build, but still, give yourself the time and space to do so.

Mind Change is not for the timid. It is for the brave. The few people ready to "take on" everything they think they know and turn it upside down will tap into a power that they only dreamed possible. The hardest and best knowledge we must face is that we have a choice.

INTRODUCTION

In the following chapters, we will lay out a step-by-step plan to help you change your mind! This handbook will cover the following:

Mind Change Manifesto

This will help you identify exactly what you would like to see in your future so that you can know where you are going. This is arguably the MOST important step of the Mind Change process!

Mind Change GPS

This will be your "directions" and tools to get you where you are going. We will teach you how to utilize your Gratitude, Positive Affirmations, and Smiles (Happy Memories) to begin creating your dreams.

Safe Haven

Having a "safe haven" that we can visit anytime, anywhere, is an extremely valuable tool. Learn how to create and use this technique to help provide a safe place for change.

PaNE CuRe List

This is a powerful tool that will help you identify the past negative experiences, limiting beliefs, and the programs that are keeping you stuck in some of your unpleasant patterns.

Pattern Interrupts

Learning this tool, and the power behind it, is a key piece to overcoming the things holding you back.

Though everyones journey and timeframe for change will be unique to them, if you apply yourself wholeheartedly to these methods and techniques, they can provide the fastest route to change I have ever encountered.

> *"I'm trying to free your mind, Neo. But I can only show you the door. You're the one that has to walk through it."*
> *- Morpheus: The Matrix*

INTRODUCTION

MIND CHANGE

MANIFESTO

Whatever we plant in our subconscious mind and nourish with repetition and emotion will one day become a reality.
-Jim Rohn

The Mind Change Manifesto helps you identify precisely what you would like to see in your future so that you know where you are going. Think of this document as if it holds magical powers. What you write can come true. So don't hold back! This a story written by you, with details, images, sounds, feelings, and character development. It is a work in progress that can be refined, fine-tuned, and upgraded. It can have pictures, poems, quotes, cards — anything you want that makes you feel good and helps you get a clearer vision of your future. Use words that inspire and are powerfully positive. If you find resistance coming to the surface as you do your Manifesto, that's ok. Just flip over to the Limiting Beliefs Section (p.83) and jot down what comes up. Only include what you DO want in your Manifesto, no negative words allowed. Our words have immense power.

--- REMEMBER ---

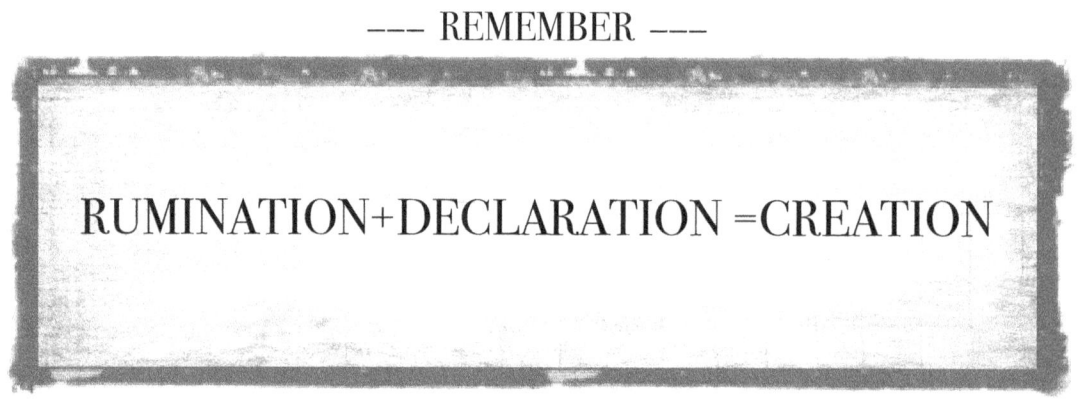

RUMINATION+DECLARATION =CREATION

Your Manifesto may include (but is not limited to) the following questions. Take a minute to explore your answers to these answers and jot down what comes up for you.

Who would I be if I were the best me?

Step out of yourself and see yourself as you'd LIKE to be. This can include character traits, feelings, attributes. If you were the best person you knew, what would you be like?

What would I do if I succeeded in every venture?

Dare to imagine yourself as a success in everything you do. Try envisioning yourself as a perpetual success. How would this change your dreams?

How do I choose to serve others and provide value to every relationship?

Giving to others and feeling valued go hand in hand. Create situations that will be a win/win for both parties.

What relationships do I already have that support and value my vision?

Think about people who "have your back". Even if they are no longer living, see yourself through their eyes. Notice how they already believe in you and can help you go even further.

What skills do I already possess that can get me closer to attaining my goals and objectives?

It's a good idea and practice to reflect on your life with the intent of finding tools and skills that you have already attained, and then recognize how you can use those to get even more.

If I had a magic wand and could have anything and everything I desired, what would I have?

Don't limit yourself to tangible ways of achieving things. We will often unknowingly limit ourselves because our reality is so restricted. Allow yourself the freedom to "magically" get things. That way, you can see an unrestricted version of what you want.

If I woke up every morning feeling the best I ever have, what would that feel like?

Be specific on the visual and "feeling" of this scenario. What would you do if you woke up every day like this? How would your life change?

What is great about my life now and what would I want to make it even better?

The power of gratitude cannot be underestimated. This practice alone will make huge strides in feeling better about your life. Taking your gratitude and using it to make more gratitude is an essential "life hack"!

IF I HAD A GREAT AND LOVING CHILDHOOD, AND EVERYONE WAS DOING THE BEST THEY COULD, WHAT WOULD IT HAVE BEEN LIKE?

This question holds the key to healing so many hurts and pains. Even if you believe you had a horrific childhood, give yourself a moment to see it differently. If your parents really were doing the best job they could (and they likely were, even if it was awful), find some of the wonderful treasures that you may have overlooked in the past. Write a story as if you had the childhood that you wished you had. Be specific about what you would have wanted. Remember, write as if you *already* have it.

WRITING YOUR MANIFESTO

Now it is time to write your Manifesto. Using some of the information that you wrote in the previous pages, begin to write the story of "where you are going". How you do this is UP TO YOU!! Some people like to do a month-out Manifesto, then a year-out Manifesto, then a 5-year Manifesto, and even a 10-year Manifesto. Don't worry about getting it "just right". You have plenty of time and can re-write the story EVEN BETTER whenever you want! This is an organic document. It is meant to be flexible. It will grow and change, just like you! As you start to attract more and more of the things on your list, you will be able to adjust and dream bigger. The only limitations are those that you impose....so don't hold back. When you begin, write this story AS IF it is already happening NOW at a future date of your choice. Here is a sample of how this may begin:

It is now January 1, 20— and I am feeling amazing. I am surrounded by supportive friends and family and I feel more loved, supported and connected than ever before. My business is incredibly successful, easily and effortlessly bringing in 2 million dollars of profit a year. My body is healthy. I am fit, lean, and strong. Each morning, I wake up early, meditate, exercise, and feed by body nutritious food so that I am ready to have an AMAZING day…..

Okay! It's time for you to get started. Have fun and dream big.

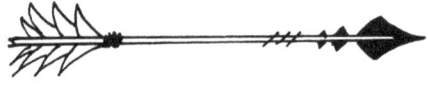

The best way to predict the future is to create it.

-Abraham Lincoln

Manifesto

Manifesto

Manifesto

Manifesto

Manifesto

Manifesto

Manifesto

Manifesto

Manifesto

MIND CHANGE

G. P. S.

"Gratitude makes sense of our past, brings peace for today, and creates a vision for tomorrow."
- Melody Beattie

Now that you have your Mind Change Manifesto, you are clearer on where you are going. Now, you need to recognize the tools you have to get there. This is where the Mind Change GPS comes into play. A GPS gives us all the tools to arrive at our desired destination. What will be included in your GPS?

"G": GRATITUDE — This can be a daily list of things that you are grateful for. Even entering 5 items every day can be a powerful tool toward getting more of what you want in life.

"P": POSITIVE AFFIRMATIONS — These can be little quotes, sayings, or purposeful affirmations that are being used to build you up. Rehearse these. Write them daily and read them aloud if possible.

"S": SMILES — This is ANYTHING that makes you smile! This can be photos, song lyrics, funny little stories, or observations. You can also glue in cards, notes, letters, or other little mementos that bring a smile to your face.

Ideally, this will include happy memories from your past, things you have loved or been inspired by in the past (or present) and will also serve as something you can add to daily. Noticing the blessings about even minor topics can help you reinforce gratitude in your life. Even something as simple as gratitude for the sun streaming through the window can be a powerful practice. Remember, **everything is a skill**. Even happiness!

Gratitude and the "record-keeping" of blessings have been studied and researched for many years. Gratitude builds on itself. Researchers note that daily practice is superior to weekly practice. The brain changes with experience, so the more often gratitude is focused on, the more the brain learns to tune in to the positive things in the world. Though it may take a little extra effort, the payoff can hardly be downplayed. Make an effort to record *at least* 3-5 things you are grateful for daily.

Gratitude

Gratitude

Gratitude

Gratitude

Gratitude

Gratitude

Gratitude

Gratitude

Gratitude

Affirmations

Did you know that an affirmation is anything we repeat or affirm? Unfortunately, we *negatively* affirm all of the time. Re-training your mind to affirm *positively* is an incredible tool!

Below is a list of common positive beliefs or affirmations. As you begin to identify negative beliefs in later sections, these positive affirmations will be within your grasp and they will become a new and wonderful identity!

RESPONSIBILITY/SELF-WORTH

I deserve love	I am a good person
I am fine as I am	I am worthy
I am honorable	I am lovable
I am deserving	I deserve good things
I can have_____	I can be healthy
I am significant	I am intelligent
I deserve to live	I am OK as I am
I did the best I could	I deserve to be happy
I can learn	I do the best I can

RELATIONSHIPS

I communicate openly with others

I resolve conflicts with respect

I share emotional intimacy with others

I am the best friend anyone can have

I choose friends who love me the way I am

The people I love approve of me

I am happy I am part of my family

I enjoy activities and celebrations with my family

I love unconditionally

I am unconditionally loved

CONFIDENCE

I am confident, enthusiastic, and energetic

My personality shows I am confident

I attract confident people

I love change

I easily adjust to new people and situations

I am outgoing and make friends easily

I am happy with myself the way I am

I am proud of myself

My self-esteem and confidence increases each day

SAFETY

I am safe

I trust my judgement

All life loves and supports me

I safely show my emotions

All is well in my world

I make my needs known

I feel divinely protected

Safety surrounds me

I am trusted

I am secure

I am loved

I easily let go

It's over now

SUCCESS

Every day I become more successful

I feel powerful, capable, and confident

I easily find solutions to problems

My work environment is calm and productive

I love learning new things and using them in my life

I am experiencing wealth every day

I am living the life of my dreams

I am financially successful in all my endeavors

I have all the time, money, and love that I need

PHYSICAL HEALTH

All my body systems function perfectly

My personality shows I am confident

Every part of my body is healthy and full of energy

I stay healthy and my immune system is very strong

I enjoy strengthening my body with exercise

I feed my body only nutritious food

I pay attention and listen to what my body tells me

I sleep soundly each night, awaking rested and refreshed

I surround myself with healthy people

My body is full of energy and vitality

MENTAL HEALTH

All of my thoughts and feelings are under control

I awake each day with excitement

I await the good things coming to me

I breathe in and out, releasing all stress

I easily forgive myself and others

I observe my emotions with peace and grace

I meditate with joy and love

My thoughts are positive and uplifting

My mind and body are perfectly aligned

I feel feelings of love, peace, and joy

Affirmations

Affirmations

Affirmations

Affirmations

Affirmations

Affirmations

Affirmations

Affirmations

Affirmations

Affirmations

Smiles

This is the section where you will begin to record your Happy Memories! Research suggests that the recalling of positive events can promote mental health resilience. Reminiscing about happy events can increase positive feelings and therefore hinder the release of stress hormones.

When I first started my healing journey, I had a very difficult time recalling "a happy memory". I made the assumption that I couldn't find any happy childhood memories because I had a rotten childhood! I was SO wrong. Yes, some not-so-wonderful things happened when I was a child.

But what I eventually realized was that I was representing my entire childhood based on about 18-20 memories that I COULD recall. And they were ALL negative. No wonder I was so miserable. If you remember from *Mind Change*, the subconscious mind (where we store memory) is the "Smart Dummy". Meaning that it is highly intelligent because it basically keeps us alive! Regulating our breathing, digestion, heart rate, and so on. But it is "dumb" in the sense that it doesn't "judge." When the subconscious mind is attempting to protect you during difficult times of your life, it will often block out entire *timeframes* or periods of time if it contains a traumatic event.

So if you were 5 years old and had an AMAZING birthday party, full of presents, fun, and love...but then at the very end of the party, you peed in your pants because you were having too much fun to stop and go to the bathroom, what part of this memory are you more likely to hold on to? The part where all your friends (who for the majority of the time were supporting and loving) are now standing around pointing and laughing. Because they are 5 YEARS OLD!!! And pee is funny (when it's not you). The traumatic nature of that event will often result in the subconscious mind "blocking" the majority of the party and focusing in ONLY on the part that makes you feel bad. Why? So that it never happens again.

The result of this kind of mechanism is that we have a much easier time recalling the negative experiences in our life. BUT...we can re-train our brain to get really good at recalling *positive* events from our history. That is an extra gift in this process!

When I finally dealt with a few of the negative memories that I was playing, and replaying FOR YEARS...it unlocked a vault of happy times from my childhood. Amazing, right? The key is, "practice makes perfect". That is what the following pages are for. So let's get started!

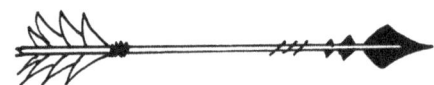

In these pages, you will record ANYTHING that makes you smile! This can be photos, song lyrics, funny little stories, or observations, as well as happy memories from any point in your life. You can also glue in cards, notes, letters, or other little mementos that bring a smile to your face.

This is also the place you will record your memory re-writes. When you use the Mind Change Method to change a memory, write the new memory in these pages. Remember to get specific. Make it good!

Happy Memory Tip

Schedule time with a friend or family member. Set the expectations for this meeting before getting together. Tell the other person that you are going to meet up and ONLY share 3-5 of your happiest memories with each other. The other rule is that there can be NO negativity or partially happy memories.

Example: "I have a great memory of sitting on my grandfathers lap and sharing homemade toffee while we watched Wizard of Oz. But then he died the next day!!!"

Nope! Only the good stuff. Remember to use emotion languaging when you are sharing your memories. "It made me feel loved and protected", "I was overcome with joy", "It made me think that I could do anything and feel invincible."

Smiles

Smiles

Smiles

Smiles

Smiles

Smiles

Smiles

Smiles

Smiles

Smiles

MIND CHANGE

SAFE HAVEN

Safe Haven

Anyone who has experienced trauma of any kind can likely explain the importance of "feeling safe" in any given situation. For people who have spent any extended period of time in a "flight/fight/freeze" response, finding a calm, safe environment can be a key to healing.

For this exercise, we capitalize on the knowledge that our mind doesn't know the difference between "happening now" and "already happened" if we are deeply rehearsing the memory. Having a "safe haven" that we can visit anytime, anywhere, is a valuable tool.

This exercise will be easier for some than others, but I encourage you to keep working on it.

Remember to include all of the sensory categories. SEE it clearly. Make all the colors brighter and the images sharper. FEEL it deeply. Practice feeling all the wonderful feelings of being in your "safe place". In mine, I can *feel* the warmth of the cup of coffee in my hand, the sun on my face, and the cool breeze coming off of the mountain. HEAR it clearly. Listen for the peaceful tones and all the little sounds that go along with your visions. KNOW what this place evokes in your mind. What are the mantras that repeat in your mind as you are in this place. "I am safe", "I am loved", "I am at peace." One of mine is, "I have nothing to do, nowhere to be, I'm free to stay as long as I like." If you would also like to add SMELLS and TASTES that are pleasing and joyful, do it! This is YOUR place, make it good.

And yes…you can have more than one!!

Safe Haven Tip

Many people have asked about having other people in your Safe Haven. My advice is to make sure it is somewhere you feel completely peaceful alone…then you can invite others in when you feel like it! Feeling peaceful and fulfilled when we are alone with ourselves is a valuable skill!

Safe Haven

Safe Haven

Safe Haven

Safe Haven

Safe Haven

Safe Haven

MIND CHANGE

PaNE CuRe

Past Negative Experiences & Current Realities

PaNE CuRe

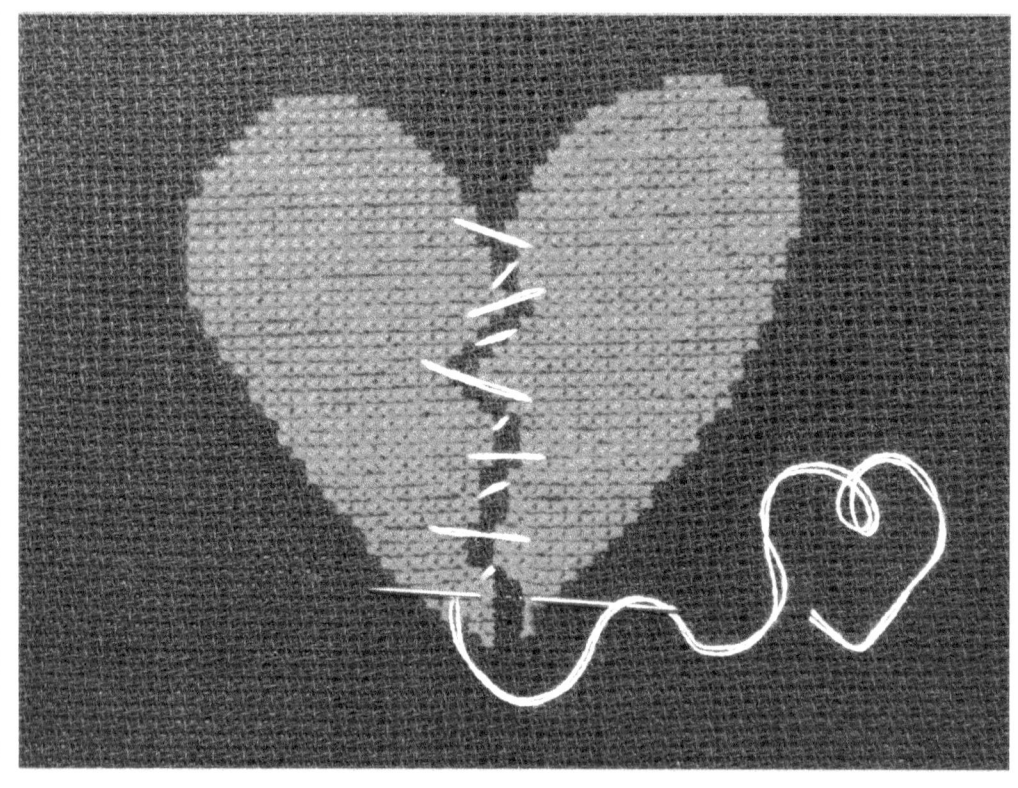

This is a powerful tool that will help you identify the past negative experiences, limiting beliefs, and programs that are keeping you stuck in some of your unpleasant patterns. It's time to go back and take inventory of the beliefs, memories, and experiences that helped you become who you are right now.

"You can't change what you don't acknowledge."
— Dr. Phil

We have become experts at not dealing with trauma. Instead, we "cope." We often equate "not feeling it" or "not thinking about it" as dealing with something. If it doesn't bother me, it doesn't exist. The problem is that it doesn't bother us because we don't acknowledge it; the "it" is the unpleasant feelings, experiences, thoughts, or past.

Consciously, we can avoid thinking about those negative experiences. But subconsciously, they are alive and well and usually gaining momentum. Remember, it's our subconscious that dictates our daily thoughts, attitudes, and behaviors. It's automatic — the inevitable out-put of what we have input over time.

Unfortunately, no amount of positive thought, positive affirmations, yoga, drugs, booze, sex, or makeup can cover these up forever. Some of these things seem to help, even for long periods. But it always shows up somewhere. As much as we would like to keep "the past in the past," if there are PNEs that need to be processed and resolved, they will keep showing up in different areas of our life.

At Mind Change, we don't run from the past. We don't talk about it until you are tired of hearing about it. We don't ignore it, and we certainly don't judge it. We change it! Well, technically, YOU change it....we facilitate the process.

You may experience a range of emotions when considering this task. Some people are very excited, knowing that identifying the "building blocks" of our experiences, beliefs, and realities is the first step in changing them. Others may feel like this task is daunting. Please give yourself ample time to finish the list.

You do not have to do it all in one sitting. Please give yourself a specific time frame each day that you will work on it. You may find that you desire to continue after the allotted time. That's fine—keep going until you are finished or feel ready to stop for the day. Otherwise, work on it for 10, 20, 30, or 60 minutes, and then stop. Pick it back up the next day.

There will be a temptation to be very emotionally involved in this list. As you are writing the list, it is crucial to remember THIS IS NOT HAPPENING NOW. You are safe. Take this opportunity to learn to be an observer. Yes, these things happened, and you have many thoughts, feelings, and sensations surrounding them. We will deal with all of that. But for now, we are merely recording them for future use.

Also, this would be an excellent time to have your Mind Change GPS handy. If, at any point, you feel that you are becoming emotionally "triggered" by making the list, take a break, and look at your GPS. Alternatively, have some funny YouTube videos handy. Whatever makes you uncontrollably happy!

Making The List

Now you are ready to make your list. Prepare yourself to do this by first sitting down and taking ten deep breaths. Breathing in through your nose and out through your mouth, try to match your inhale to a three-count beat (breathing in for three counts) and exhaling to a four-count beat. When you have completed your breathing, take a moment to invite your subconscious mind to bring forth the information that is needed. You can do this by verbally or mentally acknowledging that you are providing a safe and loving space for this process. When you are ready, you may record this information on the pages that follow.

Starting from birth, or before that, if applicable, list every PNE (perceived negative experience) in your life. You will give the memory a short title and then list 2-3 emotions, feelings, or sensations generated by this memory. You will also rate the emotional intensity of this memory next to the title using a scale of 0-10. 0 being you feel nothing and 10 being the worst feeling, as if it's happening now.

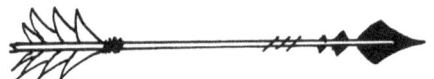

Below are detailed instructions on getting started:

List any pre-birth or ancestral trauma

These will be stories you were told, or family identities. Stories about parents or grandparents, aunts or uncles. Anything that you remember that was an unpleasant trait or story from your ancestry. You may have developed pictures in your mind or have audio recordings of the stories you were told (even if you were not even born yet.). This can even be stories about the kind of people your ancestors were, or your grandparents, or parents. If adopted, list any known or suspected circumstances of the birth parents.

Example: My grandfather was a holocaust survivor.

Title the memory, give it a rating and list any related feelings, emotions or physical sensations associated.

- Holocaust stories: (8)   fear, anger, rejection

List any birth stories

This will be stories around your birth or conception that you perceive as negative. Difficult labors, hardships, difficulty of mom getting pregnant.

Example:
Mother nearly died in labor: (6)   shame, blame, fear

Chronologically list all other PNEs

It may be helpful to divide your life into time periods (0-5 years old, 6-10 years old, etc.). Consider each time period and try to list 10 or more events. If you remember a specific event but do not have an emotional intensity with it, list it anyway. Title the memory, give it a rating, and list any related feelings, emotions, or physical sensations associated.

List all Current Realities or Core Beliefs

This will be all the negative and/or unproductive things you believe about your life now. Mantras, negative affirmations, negative "voice in your head", irrational worries, reoccurring dreams, etc.

List any "Unmentionables"

These will be things that you feel are too difficult to deal with, things you have never told anyone, family secrets, or things that you aren't sure really happened. For these, the titles can be unrelated. For example, someone who remembers an incest incident but has never talked about it could list that event here with a title of "Lemonade". Lemonade may have something or nothing to do with the actual event, but serves as a title for this particular memory.

If you suspect something happened to you, but you have no memory of it, you can make-up a short version of what might have happened and then title it. You don't have to have a conscious construct of a memory to change it. Your subconscious mind already knows.

Buried traumas that are very sensitive in nature may require the assistance of a trained professional (incest, ritual abuse, extreme physical/sexual abuse). Please don't attempt this on your own, especially if you find a good deal of emotional charge.

EVENTS TO INCLUDE AND CONSIDER

- Ancestral Identities/Stories: Wars, cultural tragedies, hardships, etc.
- How siblings & family members felt about you, how they treated you
- School experiences: bullying, shaming, embarrassments, nicknames
- Any sexual abuse or molestation
- First sexual experience: pornography, experimenting, photos/movies
- Emotional or physical abuse
- Religious traumas
- Major moves, changing schools
- Deaths of pets, pet injuries, losses
- Any romantic relationships: especially first boyfriend/girlfriend
- Pivotal points in life with parents, siblings, bosses, co-workers, etc.
- Divorce, relationship breakups, broken friendships, grief & loss: Deaths, loss of job, loss of health, loss of identity
- All hurts: anything you felt bad about when it happened
- All major medical illnesses, chronic illnesses, other medical problems
- Accidents & injuries
- Fears/Phobias: list each experience to support the fear
- Re-occurring beliefs or mantras: "You're not good enough", "You'll never amount to anything", "You are stupid", "I'm always broke", etc.

LIMITING BELIEFS

Next is a list of common limiting beliefs (also known as negative cognitions) that people have. The counterpart list of positive beliefs or affirmations can be found in the GPS section. You may want to circle any relevant beliefs to add to your PaNE CuRe. Remember, these are only suggestions. We encourage you to dig deep and see which beliefs fit your model of thinking.

SELF DEFECTIVENESS

I DON'T DESERVE LOVE	I AM A BAD PERSON
I AM TERRIBLE	I AM UNWORTHY
I AM SHAMEFUL	I AM UNLOVABLE
I AM UGLY	I AM NOT GOOD ENOUGH
I DO NOT DESERVE _____	I AM STUPID
I AM INSIGNIFICANT	I DESERVE TO BE MISERABLE
I DESERVE TO DIE	I AM A DISAPPOINTMENT
I DON'T BELONG	I WILL ALWAYS BE THIS WAY
THERE'S SOMETHING WRONG WITH ME	I AM PERMANENTLY DAMAGED

SAFETY/VULNERABILITY

I CANNOT BE TRUSTED

I CANNOT TRUST ANYONE

I CANNOT PROTECT MYSELF

IT'S NOT OK TO SHOW EMOTIONS

PEOPLE TAKE ADVANTAGE OF ME

I CANNOT STAND UP FOR MYSELF

THE WORLD IS AN UNSAFE PLACE

IF I LET IT GO, IT WILL HAPPEN AGAIN

PEOPLE ARE DANGEROUS

PEOPLE WILL USE ME

PEOPLE ARE OUT TO GET ME

I CANNOT TRUST MYSELF

I CANNOT LET IT OUT

I CANNOT TRUST MY JUDGMENT

I AM IN DANGER

VULNERABILITY IS WEAKNESS

RESPONSIBILITY/POWER

I DID SOMETHING WRONG

I SHOULD HAVE KNOWN BETTER

I SHOULD HAVE DONE SOMETHING

NOBODY UNDERSTANDS MY STORY

SOMEONE HAS TO HELP ME

NOBODY UNDERSTANDS MY STORY

IF THEY WOULDN'T HAVE _____, I WOULDN'T_____

I CAN ONLY CHANGE IF THEY_____

I HAVEN'T HAD THE SAME OPPORTUNITIES AS OTHERS

IT'S ALL UP TO ME

IT'S ALL MY FAULT

IT'S WHO I'VE ALWAYS BEEN

NOBODY SEES ME

NOBODY HEARS ME

IT ISN'T FAIR

CONTROL/CHOICE

I am not in control

I am weak

I am a failure

I have to be perfect

I am inadequate

I don't have what it takes

Nothing ever works out for me

I've already tried, and failed

I am powerless

I cannot get what I want

I cannot succeed

I cannot stand it

I don't understand

I don't have time

I don't have the money

It's too hard

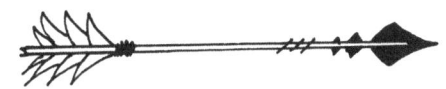

YOUR PaNE CuRe

Well done on digging into these sections! You are almost ready to do the work of Mind Change. We have provided a number of sheets for you to work on specific aspects of your PaNE CuRe. When your PaNeCuRe list is ready, have your GPS and Safe Haven close.

PaNE CuRe
(Pre-birth or ancestral trauma)

PaNE CuRe
(Birth stories)

PaNE CuRe
(Chronological PNE's)

PaNE CuRe
(Chronological PNE's)

PaNE CuRe
(Chronological PNE's)

PaNE CuRe
(Chronological PNE's)

PaNE CuRe
(Current Realities)

PaNE CuRe
(Current Realities)

PaNE CuRe
(Limiting Core Beliefs)

PaNE CuRe
("Unmentionables")

MIND CHANGE

PATTERN INTERRUPT

PATTERN INTERRUPT

A pattern interrupt is a term that comes from hypnosis and is used in Neuro-Linguistic Programming (NLP). It means to change a person's state, pattern, or trance by interruption. A pattern can be interrupted by any unexpected or sudden movement or response.

Unless you actively engage your conscious awareness, you will have an almost automatic response to most situations. Our experiences program these responses. When you Pattern Interrupt someone, they experience momentary confusion, and in some circumstances, transient amnesia. This confusion state can make you open to suggestion. We can program in another state of mind within these moments. Not only that, but with enough "interruption," we can completely scramble a well-known program, pathway, or trance.

The information feedback loop between our brain and body works very similarly to the encoding of a CD. If we understand the cyclical nature of that loop, we can use it to our advantage. When we are in an undesirable loop, we can interrupt it, like scratching a CD. Do it enough times, and it won't play any longer!

TRANCE

A little more on the "trance" concept. We are in a trance the majority of the time. With an average of up to 50,000 thoughts per day, up to 95% of those thoughts are the same thoughts we had yesterday. We then repeat those same thoughts over and over again, every day. That's a lot of practice! These have all been categorized and now are nearly automatic productions. Driving to work: Trance. Performing your work duties: Trance. Speaking with coworkers: Trance. It's the "How" you do things. Your brain already "knows how" because it does it, in some form or fashion, every day.

This is why it can seem so hard to change at times. We are keeping ourselves in the same situations, thinking the same thoughts, producing the same feelings day after day. We have a conscious awareness that we would like to be different, but we use the same resources to produce a different result. That is rarely successful. If we can be aware of these programs and make conscious efforts to interrupt those repetitive messages, then we are left open to suggestions. The brain has to recalibrate because you are introducing something unknown and unexpected into the feedback loop. Since we already have our Mind Change Manifesto, we can always suggest something in alignment with what we want for the future!"

TYPES OF PATTERN INTERRUPTS

There are countless types of Pattern Interrupts to help you change your mind. Next, I will list some examples in conjunction with each common Representational System. Used in conjunction with the other concepts, tools, and suggestions in this book, a Pattern Interrupt is an incredibly powerful tool. Remember, this is far more than just a distraction. This is an intentional effort to interrupt and corrupt any line of negative thinking. Some will work better than others. Find what works for you!

VISUAL PATTERN INTERRUPTS

- Watch a funny YouTube video
- Look through your GPS
- See the memory on an Etch-A-Sketch and slide the bar to erase
- Open your eyes and do figure 8 patterns with your eyes
- Push the image so far away in your mind, you can no longer see it
- Make a funny face in the mirror
- See the memory as a photo in your mind, now adjust the color until it's all white
- See the memory as a photo, now put it into a magicians hat, snap your fingers, and watch it disappear. Look back in the hat and see what good thing has arrived to replace it
- See all the memories you need to work on as laundry around a room. Collect each item and put it into a laundry basket. Now, do the wash. See how differently the memories come out of the wash
- Envision everyone in the memory dressed as Disney princesses. How does this change things?
- Envision everyone in the memory as if they were penguins. How does this change things?
- Envision everyone in the memory with their underwear on the outside of their clothes. How does this change things?
- Put the memory on a photo and then create another photo next to it. In this photo, create the perfect scenario. Now, overlay the "good" scenario on top of the old photo. Watch the old photo fade away
- Envision your hero showing up in the memory. How would they have changed it?
- Try to envision what it would look like to see two elephants ice-skating in pink tutus
- Try to envision two porcupines slow dancing while wearing cowboy boots
- Open your eyes and count all the blue items in your surroundings
- Open your eyes and blink along to the tune of Twinkle, Twinkle

AUDITORY PATTERN INTERRUPTS

- Listen to a favorite song
- Sing a favorite song
- Sing the SpongeBob Squarepants theme
- Speak the lyrics to a nursery rhyme
- Play a noise (fart, baby laughing, animal sounds)
- Hear what your hero or loved one would say to you instead.
- Hear the ocean waves
- If you are hearing someone say words to you that are negative, change their voice to your favorite cartoon character
- Speak positive affirmations
- Say, "I release and let go of the power I have given this memory"
- Play the words that someone is speaking to you in the memory in reverse
- Spell aloud "super-cali-fragilistic-expi-ali-docious"
- Quote your favorite movie
- Take a deep breath in and breathe out slowly with an "S" sound the whole time, making it as loud as you can
- Make beatbox sounds and try to keep the beat
- Imagine you are popping bubble wrap. What does it sound like?
- Ask your smart phone to tell you a joke
- Remember back to the first time you heard your favorite song and notice the volume and turn it up!
- Do your best impression of Kermit the frog and Miss Piggy
- Imagine there was a mute button on a negative memory. How would this change your feelings?
- Imagine your song playing in reverse
- Shout at the top of your lungs, "I am more than enough!"
- Do the Darth Vader heavy breathing voice and say "Luke, I am your father"
- Put your wrist up to your ear and listen to your pulse beating
- Gulp some water down as LOUD as you can
- Whisper "I'm safe now"

KINESTHETIC INTERRUPTS

- Stand up and turn around before sitting back down
- Do 5-10 jumping jacks / push-ups / pull-ups / squats
- Balance for 10 seconds on one foot touching your head with your fingers
- Tap your fingers together and focus on how it feels.
- Clap your hands 13 minus 6 times
- Snap your fingers to the beat of "Let it go"
- Try and move your eyebrows up and down individually
- Give yourself a shoulder rub
- Give yourself the biggest hug possible and imagine it's Santa
- Do a little dance in the mirror

AUDIO-DIGITAL INTERRUPTS

- Imagine that the conversation in your mind is being had with another (higher level) you. What insight does the other "you" have?
- What is the overall message of this memory? Notice it and write it down. Is this thought or belief one that you want more of? What would you rather believe?
- If this memory were a person, who would it be?
- If this memory had a belief what would it be?
- Can you list 3 things that might contradict the message of this memory?

** Audio/Digital representation is when we are "in our own head". It involves having a dialogue or conversation with yourself about the situation. The most helpful thing will be to step back and become aware of the conversation. Do what you need to interrupt the voice in your head.

You are ready to begin MIND CHANGE!

Next is a review of the basic Mind Change process, followed by a section you can use as you begin changing specific memories and beliefs. Most people have about 10-15 core memories that drive them to do what they do not want to do. When you shift your perception of those core memories, your entire world shifts.

MIND CHANGE PROCESS

Now, think about or recall the problem or event in detail. Notice the emotions, feelings, sounds, and/or specific images that are present in this memory. Allow it to happen as if it's happening RIGHT NOW. If it's safe to do so, step into the memory, imagine yourself really there, see what you saw, hear what you heard, and feel what you felt. This is the time to make it as strong as possible because it will only last a short amount of time. This should take you no longer than 30 seconds to 1 minute. Any longer and you begin *practicing* the feelings all over again, because the feedback loop has already been playing.

As soon as you reach this place, it's time to open your eyes and engage a **Pattern Interrupt**. The optimal Pattern Interrupt will be one that corresponds with the Representational System that you used to most fully recall this memory. For instance, if you have a mental picture of the memory (V), open your eyes and look through your GPS. Or, you can visit your mental Safe Haven. Alternatively, you can watch a quick YouTube video of funny animals. Spend 30 seconds or so in any one or more of these activities. The most important thing is to shift your focus from the memory completely (picture, feeling, sensation, sound) you are working on, to the Pattern Interrupt.

As soon as you are ready, close your eyes and take 2 deep breaths (3-4 second inhales through the nose, followed by 4-5 second exhales through the mouth). Notice that breathing brings you back to a grounded place. Now, go back and check your memory that you are working on. Notice what has changed. Notice that the intensity has lessened, or the picture has changed. Maybe the feeling has reduced or moved to another part of your body. Just notice what's left. Now, go to any part of the memory that still bothers you, notice how you know it bothers you, intensify it if you can, see what you see/feel/hear…now, Pattern Interrupt again.

RATING YOUR MEMORY

Once you've identified HOW you know this event happened, notice how much it bothers you. Now you can give the memory a rating to acknowledge how much it bothers you. Something like, on a scale of 0-10, 0 being you feel nothing at all and 10 you feel as if this is happening again right now, how much can you make this memory bother you? Write this number down beside the title on your paper.

This will be easier for some than others. That is okay. If you have a difficult time finding an accurate number, just make a guess. We ask you to rate your memories as a guide to show you the progress that is being made.

If you find that the number goes "UP" while you are working on the memory, this means that you have amplified or found additional resources to support this memory. It doesn't mean it's "getting worse". It simply means that your subconscious mind is digging up all the ways that this memory bothered you. Just notice any additional information that may arise and let it go. As the intensity of the memory decreases, notice that you are able to begin to experience the memory in a different way now.

Pictures may change. The audio may disappear or lessen. The feelings may dissipate or change to something more peaceful.

Continue to change your rating as you move through the process. Until you reach "0" (Zero). Meaning that the memory no longer bothers you. At that point, you are ready for the next step!

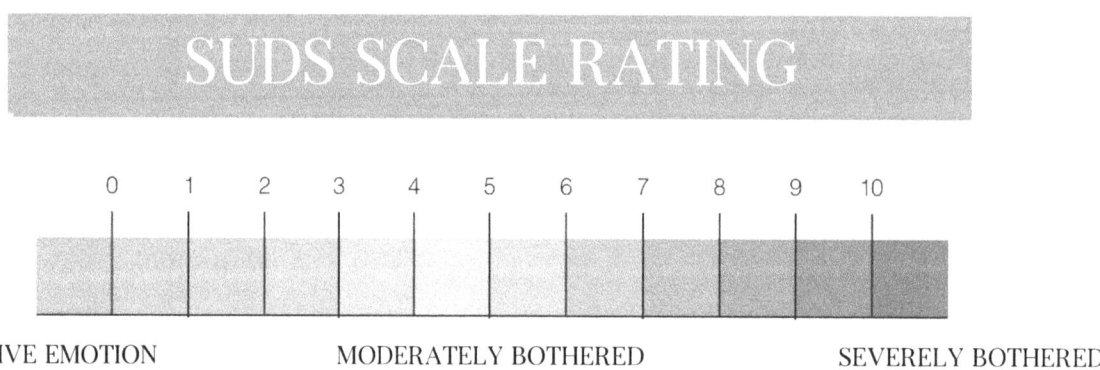

KEEP GOING UNTIL IT'S GREAT

Continue this process until the memory can no longer bother you. Once you can no longer make the memory bother you, it's time to change your mind. If the memory was primarily a picture, you may notice that the picture has already changed. The brain is amazing that way! If not, you may just notice that you can no longer find the picture, or it has gone blurry. Now is the time to be intentional about what we hold within. Ask yourself, "What would I have rather seen instead?" If auditory, "What would I have rather heard?" If kinesthetic, "What would I have rather felt?" Make it good, because you will get more of what you hold! Go back into the memory and re-decorate a bit.

If you are working on a memory and find resistance, that is okay. It doesn't mean it didn't work, it only means you have a little more investment in this belief. It may be foundational and could require one or two sessions of self work. Take a break and come back later. You may find that the memory is now changed. If not, you will likely find less resistance when you revisit it. Just think, it probably took you many years to develop such a deeply-rooted response. Or you have practiced this memory thousands of times, therefore reinforcing it daily. It may take you a few hours or even days to re-write some of these events, but it is well worth it!

A word of caution: Though this method has been used to tackle some of the most devastating traumas, it is advised that you work with a skilled practitioner if you find that the emotional charge of the memory is too high. The trance of the painful memory can sometimes be so powerful that you have a very difficult time breaking it on your own. This is where an experienced professional can utilize different protocols to break that trance. This is very deep work and it can be very beneficial to work with someone who has been trained to handle any situation that may arise.

It is the ultimate goal of any Mind Change practitioner to empower the client to work on themselves eventually. So starting out with a practitioner can be very beneficial.

For those of you interested in scheduling sessions, learning more, becoming a practitioner, or attending a live training, please visit the Mind Change website at www.MindChange.com for more information.

A COUPLE MORE THINGS

As you are working through your list, you may encounter some "bumps" in the road. That is totally normal, and to be expected. Here are a couple of things that might show up.

Secondary Gains

These are any subconscious "benefits" of our problems that keep our limiting beliefs in place. Remember, these typically don't "make sense" to us on a conscious level. But the subconscious mind makes these logical connections from our past, based on experience.

Example #1: When I have a migraine, people don't expect me to do anything. So I finally get that break I need so badly.

Example #2: When I am overweight, I don't attract male attention. Therefore I am safe from unwanted advances.

Example #3: I have already failed so many times, I will probably do it again. So if I sabotage this great job opportunity *now*, I won't have to suffer the humiliation of a larger failure down the road.

Remember, the goal of your subconscious mind is to keep you safe. If we can identify some of the potential benefits, or secondary gains within a limiting belief, we can train our subconscious minds that it's safe to do something else.

Resistance

It is common to find resistance whenever you attempt to change beliefs. If you find resistance, that is okay. It can even be good. Resistance is a good indicator of investment. It is good to see what beliefs you are really invested in.

Resistance can show up in many different ways.

- Lack of motivation to work on yourself
- Memories refusing to change
- Getting sleepy, sick, or agitated when you begin to work
- Not being able to "find" the memories
- Overcomplicating the Mind Change process
- Not making the time to do the work
- And more....

If you find resistance, there are a few ways to handle it:
- You can acknowledge it as resistance, thank it for coming (as a safety mechanism) and mentally include it in what you are working on.
- You can work on the resistance *before* moving on. Just use the same process for the resistance as you would for a memory. When you are finished, just go back to the memory you were originally working with.
- You can acknowledge it, thank it for showing up to protect you, and then just jot it down to deal with at a later time. Often times, just acknowledging the resistance will be enough to move past it.

Remember, it is there to "keep you safe". But that doesn't mean we need to keep doing things the same way.

On the pages to follow, we give you an example of a Mind Change Worksheet followed by blank worksheets for you to fill out and work through. This is a sample only. If it works for you, great! If you find another format that is a better fit, that is okay too. On the first example, you will see the worksheet filled out with the "problem". On the second example, you will find the same worksheet, but with the results listed as well. Again, these are just examples to get you started.

MIND CHANGE

IN ACTION!!

EXAMPLE (PART 1)

MEMORY TITLE: Bullied in 3rd Grade				
HOW (V, A, K, O, G, A/D)	**BULLET POINTS**	**RATING:**	**How I changed it!** (Write this in your GPS)	**Most Effective Pattern Interrupt Used**
V	• I can see myself on the ground with the other kids around me • I can see their angry faces • I can see tears streaming down my face and dirt on my clothes • I see the color of the blood dripping from my nose	8		
K	• I feel mad, hurt, scared, embarrassed, full of rage, wanting revenge • I feel the anger of the other children	10		
A	• I hear them shouting "Fight, Fight" • I hear laughing, shouting and the sound of the blood pumping through my body • I hear my short, fast breaths	7		
O	• I could smell the dirt and my sweat	2		
G	—	—		
A/D	• I believed I was weak • I did something wrong • People don't like me • I need protect myself • People are unsafe • Nobody protected me	7		

MIND CHANGE IN ACTION

EXAMPLE (PART 2)

MEMORY TITLE: Bullied in 3rd Grade

HOW (V, A, K, O, G, A/D)	BULLET POINTS	RATING:	How I changed it! (Write this in your GPS)	Most Effective Pattern Interrupt Used
V	• I can see myself on the ground with the other kids around me • I can see their angry faces • I can see tears streaming down my face and dirt on my clothes • I see the color of the blood dripping from my nose	8	I now see me and the group of friends playing Red Rover all together. We are all smiling, having fun, and free. We love and support each other.	Looking through my GPS
K	• I feel mad, hurt, scared, embarrassed, full of rage, wanting revenge • I feel the anger of the other children	10	I feel free and supported. The other children feel loved and supported as well. We all are grateful for the friendships that we have and feel safe to play	Jumping Jacks
A	• I hear them shouting "Fight, Fight" • I hear laughing, shouting, and the sound of the blood pumping through my body • I hear my short, fast breaths	7	I hear all of us laughing and yelling, "Red Rover, Red Rover, let Suzie come over!" I hear encouragement from all the friends.	Listening to a Baby Laughing
O	• I could smell the dirt and my sweat	2	I smell lollipops and popcorn	Visiting my Safe Haven
G	—	—		
A/D	• I believed I was weak • I did something wrong • People don't like me • I need protect myself • People are unsafe • Nobody protected me	7	This day I learned that I easily fit in and am loved I am such a good friend Friends are good and fun I am safe and protected	Repeating my positive affirmation out loud

Choosing A Memory

Either chronologically, by intensity or perceived importance, pick a memory or problem to work on. If it is a problem, take a minute to notice how you know it's a problem. Allow any pictures, feelings, or sensations to surface. You may notice that one or more memories surface. If so, notate those. Even if you think they are unrelated, just trust the subconscious mind and work through what comes up.

Write the title of this memory down (on the pages to follow). Close your eyes and GO THERE. Notice what you notice. HOW do you know this happened? Do you see pictures? Hear voices or words? Does a feeling emerge? Maybe it's a mixture of one or more. The most important part of this is knowing HOW you know.

It is important NOT to spend a great deal of time here, trying to "figure it out". Just notice HOW you know and then move on. If you find that you cannot answer "How do I know?", then just put it as a "knowing". But the more visual/kinesthetic/auditory details that you can notice, the quicker you can begin to change it.

Under the memory title, write one of the following letters:

V: If you are seeing pictures, movies or snapshots, write V (Visual) on your paper next to the title.
A: If you are hearing things within the memory, write A (Auditory) on your paper next to the title.
K: If you have feelings, sensations or emotions arise, write K (Kinesthetic) on your paper next to the title.
O: If you have smells in this memory, write O (Olfactory) on your paper next to the title.
G: If you have tastes that arise, write G (Gustatory) on your paper next to the title.
A/D: If you have an internal dialogue that you can hear or a" knowing" that it happened but nothing else, write A/D (Audio Digital) on your paper next to the title. These can also be beliefs that you developed about yourself.

(Note: you may have one or more ways you are holding this memory. Just notate all that apply).

For each letter that applied to you, write 2-3 different things you notice from that category.

Working Through Your PaNE CuRe List

Prepare yourself for each session by taking a moment of prayer or meditation and/or breathing, using this time to give thanks for the ability to do this work and for the healing that will happen. Next, choose a calm, quiet area where you will not be disturbed. Set a timer for the amount of time you would like to spend.

If you have your Safe Haven handy, this would be a great time to go there and spend a minute or so indulging in the good feelings. As you do this, engage in some deep breathing. Deep, 3-4 second inhales through the nose, followed by 4-5 second exhales through the mouth. Do this 4-5 times or until your "feel good" state is achieved.

IT'S TIME TO GET STARTED

You are ready. It's time. In the beginning, this will be unfamiliar and "clunky". Keep working at it. It gets easier. Learning to change your mind is a skill. The more you practice, the better you get.

Let's be the adventurers of our own destiny, the surveyors of our own mind. Let us make friends with our subconscious mind and begin to learn the language of our souls. If you need help, reach out. Read more. Listen more. Become an expert in the art of YOU.

We suggest that you use the following worksheets to begin to address some of the memories on your PaNE CuRe list. Beyond that, feel free to utilize the same format in the examples, or explore other options that may work for you.

Remember to FIRST fill in the "How," "Bullet Points," and "Rating." Then, after you have worked on yourself using Mind Change, fill out "How I changed it!" and the "Most Effective Pattern Interrupt Used."

In order to help you along the way, please feel free to check out our YouTube Channel and enter this unlisted video as a bonus for those who have purchased this handbook — This video is a live demonstration of how to work on yourself (please type it into your browser bar exactly as it is shown here):

https://youtu.be/0dGNbKqi5o8

Helpful Mind Change Questions To Ask Yourself

Below are a list of questions that can help you identify different aspects of the PNE in order to fully clear out the problem and change it. If you get stuck, these are great to run through to let your subconscious answer on a deeper level. Do not think about the answer before answering. Whatever comes up first is the best place to start. The final two questions can be used after you have cleaned up the issue in order to change that old story into a new and wonderful one.

- How do I know I have this problem?
- What do I believe about this problem?
- What is the worst part about this problem?
- When did this begin?
- What else was going on when this started?
- When was the first time I remember having this problem?
- Who else do I know that has this problem?
- What happens inside me when I have this problem?
- What do I see / hear / feel / taste / smell / know?
- If this was a person, who would it be?
- If this had a voice what would it say?
- If this had a message, what would it be?
- What would I rather have happened?
- How could I make this even better?

MIND CHANGE IN ACTION

MEMORY TITLE:				
HOW (V, A, K, O, G, A/D)	**BULLET POINTS**	**RATING:**	**How I changed it!** (Write this in your GPS)	**Most Effective Pattern Interrupt Used**
V				
K				
A				
O				
G				
A/D				

MIND CHANGE HANDBOOK

MEMORY TITLE:				
HOW (V, A, K, O, G, A/D)	**BULLET POINTS**	**RATING:**	**How I changed it!** (Write this in your GPS)	**Most Effective Pattern Interrupt Used**
V				
K				
A				
O				
G				
A/D				

MIND CHANGE IN ACTION

MEMORY TITLE:

HOW (V, A, K, O, G, A/D)	BULLET POINTS	RATING:	How I changed it! (Write this in your GPS)	Most Effective Pattern Interrupt Used
V				
K				
A				
O				
G				
A/D				

MIND CHANGE HANDBOOK

MEMORY TITLE:

HOW (V, A, K, O, G, A/D)	BULLET POINTS	RATING:	How I changed it! (Write this in your GPS)	Most Effective Pattern Interrupt Used
V				
K				
A				
O				
G				
A/D				

HOW (V, A, K, O, G, A/D)	BULLET POINTS	RATING:	How I changed it! (Write this in your GPS)	Most Effective Pattern Interrupt Used
MEMORY TITLE:				
V				
K				
A				
O				
G				
A/D				

MIND CHANGE HANDBOOK

MEMORY TITLE:

HOW (V, A, K, O, G, A/D)	BULLET POINTS	RATING:	How I changed it! (Write this in your GPS)	Most Effective Pattern Interrupt Used
V				
K				
A				
O				
G				
A/D				

MIND CHANGE IN ACTION

MEMORY TITLE:

HOW (V, A, K, O, G, A/D)	BULLET POINTS	RATING:	How I changed it! (Write this in your GPS)	Most Effective Pattern Interrupt Used
V				
K				
A				
O				
G				
A/D				

MIND CHANGE HANDBOOK

MEMORY TITLE:

HOW (V, A, K, O, G, A/D)	BULLET POINTS	RATING:	How I changed it! (Write this in your GPS)	Most Effective Pattern Interrupt Used
V				
K				
A				
O				
G				
A/D				

MIND CHANGE IN ACTION

MEMORY TITLE:

HOW (V, A, K, O, G, A/D)	BULLET POINTS	RATING:	How I changed it! (Write this in your GPS)	Most Effective Pattern Interrupt Used
V				
K				
A				
O				
G				
A/D				

MIND CHANGE HANDBOOK

MEMORY TITLE:

HOW (V, A, K, O, G, A/D)	BULLET POINTS	RATING:	How I changed it! (Write this in your GPS)	Most Effective Pattern Interrupt Used
V				
K				
A				
O				
G				
A/D				

MIND CHANGE IN ACTION

HOW (V, A, K, O, G, A/D)	BULLET POINTS	RATING:	How I changed it! (Write this in your GPS)	Most Effective Pattern Interrupt Used
MEMORY TITLE:				
V				
K				
A				
O				
G				
A/D				

MIND CHANGE HANDBOOK

MEMORY TITLE:

HOW (V, A, K, O, G, A/D)	BULLET POINTS	RATING:	How I changed it! (Write this in your GPS)	Most Effective Pattern Interrupt Used
V				
K				
A				
O				
G				
A/D				

MEMORY TITLE:				
HOW (V, A, K, O, G, A/D)	**BULLET POINTS**	**RATING:**	**How I changed it!** (Write this in your GPS)	**Most Effective Pattern Interrupt Used**
V				
K				
A				
O				
G				
A/D				

MIND CHANGE

BONUS

Re-Write Your Childhood

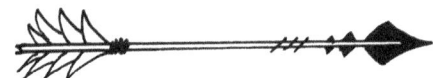

This is a little bonus section that can be extremely powerful for your life. Our childhoods have a profound effect on our current behaviors and realties. Some people may balk at this exercise, thinking that our past is "in our past" and cannot be changed. I found this to be untrue. For me, I was so focused on the negative memories that I was holding on to, that I had neglected the majority of the positive memories. When I cleared up many of those negative references, I was free to experience my childhood in a completely different way.

If memory is…unreliable at best, it's safe to say that a large portion of our past had already been changed. Our repeated accessing of those memories, by our perceptions as we mature, and by the particular events we choose to focus on. So if most of our past is "made-up" anyway, shouldn't we make-it-up in a good way? If you are going to tell yourself stories (especially if they have a direct effect on your current behavior), make sure you are telling yourself good ones!!

BONUS

This is your chance to rewrite the "childhood of your dreams". Like the question in the Manifesto section, this is a chance to elaborate on how good things would be if everyone in your life as a child was living from their higher self.

If you find resistance to this, add that to your PaNE CuRe list and work it out! Allow your parents the opportunity to parent in the best way possible. Allow your siblings to be as supportive and encouraging they could be. If you were an only child, let that be a great experience for you in every way.

If there is anyone in your immediate family, or close family that you need to make peace with, clean that up in your PaNE CuRe list and let them live their best self HERE in your story.

Some of you had great childhoods, and that is wonderful! Write out all the amazing reasons why! Could it have been EVEN BETTER?!? Write that story too. Don't hold back. The "little you" deserves every good thing. Go back and set that child free!

Ready, Set, Go!!!

MIND CHANGE HANDBOOK

BONUS

BONUS

MIND CHANGE HANDBOOK

Congratulations!

CONGRATULATIONS

Well Done! You did it! This is another step in the journey to your BEST LIFE. Come on…admit it…you are even more awesome than before. Am I right? You have just added incredibly powerful tools to your "toolbox of life" that will continue to empower you throughout journey. Keep doing the work. We are never really done. Life keeps happening, so we need to keep being intentional about creating it. If this journal is full, get another one! Or make your own. Just keep them going.

Share this with others! We would love to see a photo of you with your journal. Post a picture on social media and tag us **@MindChangeMethod** — Spread the love and encouragement. Goodness knows the world needs as much hope, change, and positivity as it can get.

Thank you for investing in YOU. Thank you for doing the work and healing the past hurts in your life. Don't worry if there are more. You have the power to change it now. You are now clearer on who you are, what you want to create in life, and the direction you want to go in. We are sending you lots of light, love, and peace on the next stage of your path. Keep us in the loop!

May many more successes and victories be yours.
Peace and Aloha,

EXTRA NOTES

EXTRA NOTES

EXTRA NOTES

EXTRA NOTES

EXTRA NOTES

www.ingramcontent.com/pod-product-compliance
Lightning Source LLC
Chambersburg PA
CBHW081229080526
44587CB00022B/3873